# THE
# BEAD MAKER

# THE
# BEAD MAKER

Mary Maguire

NORTH LIGHT BOOKS

First published in Great Britain in 2002 by
Collins & Brown Limited
64 Brewery Road
London N7 9NT

A member of **Chrysalis** Books plc

First published in North America
in 2002 by North Light Books
an imprint of F&W Publications
4700 East Galbraith Road
Cincinnati, Ohio 45236

9 8 7 6 5 4 3 2 1

British Library Cataloguing-in-Publication Data: A catalogue record for
this book is available from the British Library

ISBN: 1-58180-304-4

Project managed by Emma Baxter
Designed by Anne-Marie Bulat
Photography by Siân Irvine
Copy-edited by Michelle Pickering

Color reproduction by Classicscan, Singapore
Printed by Kyodo Printing Co (Singapore) Pte Ltd

# contents

# introduction

This book demonstrates how to make fabulous beads using many different materials and employing a wide variety of techniques. Whatever your level of skill, there is something here for you.

The main body of the book is divided into eight chapters, defined by the materials used: formers, self-hardening clay, polymer clay, felt, paper, natural materials, aromatics, plastic, and embroidery.

## techniques & projects

There is a techniques section at the beginning of each chapter with photographic step-by-step guidelines for making and embellishing beads using that particular material.

The chapter then features several projects that you can make yourself. There are beautiful atmospheric photographs of the finished beads, lists of the materials and tools required, and detailed descriptions of how the beads are made.

## sourcing materials

All of the materials used to make the beads in this book are inexpensive, and some cost nothing at all. Most of them are readily available from good craft stores. If you do not have a supplier near you, use the handy list of resources at the back of the book to find companies that operate a mail-order system.

## simple & challenging

The pleasure you will get from making your own beads is well worth the effort involved. Start with simple beads, such as the rolled paper beads on pages 60–61. These particular beads were made with special origami paper, but any paper will do. You can even use paper grocery bags or scraps of wallpaper. The results can be surprising. This is also a good project

make them for someone else—handmade necklaces, bracelets, and earrings make very handsome gifts.

The chapter describes the various findings that are available for turning beads into pieces of jewelry and gives advice on which to use. It also shows how you can use beads to make items such as light pulls and tassels.

## have fun!

The most important thing about making beads is that you enjoy the process. It is a joyful craft that can easily be done at a kitchen table. Use the book as inspiration, and once you have mastered the techniques involved, create your own beads by adapting and elaborating on the recipes shown here. There are myriad possibilities just waiting to be discovered.

to make with children, as are the self-hardening clay beads in chapter two.

Then progress through the book to the more challenging beads, such as the complex canes of millefiore in chapter three and the machine-embroidered beads in chapter nine.

## using your beads

The final chapter of the book explains the different ways in which you can use your beads. You can transform them into beautiful pieces of jewelry to complement a special outfit, or

Mary Maguire

using
formers

# former techniques

Readymade base beads—formers—can be bought from craft stores or you can make your own. They can be embellished in many ways.

**Buying formers** Base beads are available in many different materials, including styrofoam, paper, acrylic, and wood. They can be bought unpainted or in various colors, or made from scratch.

### ENCRUSTED BEADS

**1 Making formers** Roll a piece of air-drying modeling clay between your palms to the required size. Pierce with a darning needle, then thread the former onto a wooden skewer.

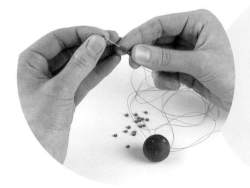

**4 Encrusting** Allowing 1tsp of seed beads per former, mix 1tsp of waterproof craft glue with 2tsp of seed beads. Smooth the beads over a small area of the former at a time using a popsicle stick to ensure even distribution. Allow to dry, removing the stick just before they have dried thoroughly.

### WRAPPING BEADS

**1 Anchoring** Thread a needle with 3' (1m) of thread. Tie a small bead that is slightly larger than the hole in the former onto the end of the thread, then insert the needle through the former so that the bead acts as an anchor. Thread lots of seed beads onto the needle.

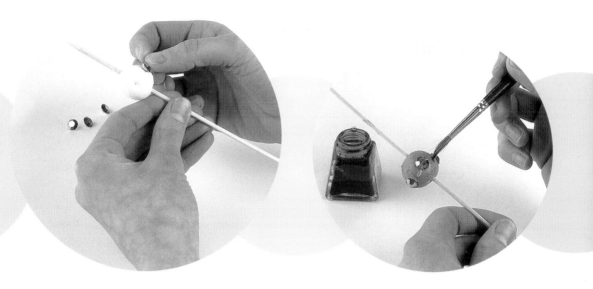

**2 Embedding** Before the former has dried, press gems into the clay at regular intervals (do not use flat-backed gems). Remove the gems and allow the former to dry. When it is ready, fix the gems into place with two-part epoxy glue and allow to dry.

**3 Painting** Paint the former in a suitable color. For example, if you plan to encrust the former with red seed beads, paint it with a red base color. Use a fine artist's brush and waterproof ink.

**2 Gluing and spiraling** Spread fast-drying glue over the top quarter of the former (at the opposite end to the anchor bead), then wrap the beaded thread in a spiral around the hole in the former. Press to make sure the beads are in contact with the glue. Allow to dry. Repeat until you reach halfway.

**3 Finishing off** Cut off the anchor bead. Repeat the gluing and spiraling process until the former is three-quarters and then completely covered. Allow to dry. Cut off the remaining thread and tuck the end of the thread inside the embellished former.

# snowballs

These exuberant, bubbly beads are great fun to make and wear. Use them to make necklaces, bracelets, and earrings and they will help break the ice at any social occasion.

Roll a small piece of clay between your palms until it is round and of the required size. Pierce a hole through the former with a darning needle and thread it onto a wooden skewer (if you want to make several snowball beads, you can usually fit around four formers onto the wooden skewer at once). Allow the former to harden.

Mix your seed beads with waterproof craft glue in a ratio of 2tsp of beads to 1tsp of glue. Using a popsicle stick, spread the mixture over the top half of the former, smoothing the beads evenly across its surface. Allow to dry and repeat on the opposite side.

Once the surface of the former has lost its tackiness, but before the glue has completely dried, remove the stick by twisting it slowly out with one hand while supporting the former around the stick with your other hand. If some of the seed beads became dislodged, replace them with more of the same mixture. Allow to dry thoroughly before using the finished snowball bead.
(For additional help with this project refer to Encrusted beads, *page 10–11.*)

## materials

air dry modeling clay
white or transparent seed beads
waterproof craft glue

## tools

darning needle
wooden skewer
popsicle stick

**Opposite:** *White or transparent seed beads will transform a plain, clayformer into an encrusted, sparkling party bead—perfect for winter festivities. Snowballs make sensational jewelry or Christmas decorations.*

# candy-foil beads

Discarded candy foils (or wrappers) make a colorful wrapping for plain paper formers. Once glued to the surface and varnished, they make very pretty and inexpensive beads.

Pierce a hole through the paper former with a darning needle, making sure that the entry and exit holes are evenly spaced. Use a craft knife to trim off any protruding paper where the needle emerges. Thread the former onto a wooden skewer and use the end of another stick to spread a layer of glue over the former. Select some foil candy wrappers and place them in a random but pleasing pattern around the former until it is completely covered. Allow to dry.

Carefully remove the bead from the stick and glue foil over both of the holes. Allow to dry, then repierce the holes with the darning needle. Use a clean paintbrush to coat the dried former with several coats of clear gloss varnish. Allow each coat of varnish to dry thoroughly before applying the next.

## materials

paper former or similar base bead
waterproof craft glue
foil candy wrappers in a variety
  of colors
clear gloss varnish

## tools

darning needle
craft knife
2 wooden skewers
paintbrush

**Opposite:** *Keep your favorite foil candy wrappers to create these bright, sparkling beads. Not only are they great fun to make and wear, but they cost next to nothing. (See left for actual bead size.)*

# beaded baubles

These subtle beads are reminiscent of the 1930s. The tiny crystal beads have been threaded onto cotton that has then been wrapped in a spiral and glued around the base bead.

## materials

paper former or similar base bead

metallic thread

small anchor bead

transparent seed beads

## tools

darning needle

craft knife

beading needle

wooden skewer

Pierce a hole through the paper former with a darning needle, making sure that the entry and exit holes are neatly and evenly spaced. Use a craft knife to trim off any messy, protruding paper where the needle emerges.

Thread a beading needle with metallic thread and tie a small bead at the end of it (make sure the bead is larger than the hole in the former). You will need approximately 3′ (1m) of thread for a large former, and around half that length for a small one. Insert the needle and thread through the hole in the former. The small bead will act as an anchor. Thread the transparent seed beads onto the beading needle, then use the end of a wooden skewer to spread glue onto the top quarter of the former. Wrap the beaded thread in a spiral around the hole in the former, pressing gently onto the glue. When you have covered the glued portion with beads, allow to dry. Repeat the whole process of gluing and spiraling until you reach halfway down the former. Cut off the anchor bead and complete the gluing and spiraling process, taking care to keep the bead centered. When the glue is dry, pass the remaining length of unbeaded thread through the hole and cut off the excess. (For additional help with this project refer to Wrapping beads, *page 10–11.*)

**Opposite:** *The art deco bead. By using metallic thread and transparent seed beads, a plain paper former can metamorphose into a sophisticated bauble or decoration, or perhaps stylish earrings. (See left for actual bead size.)*

# bobby dazzlers

By embedding gems into your formers and surrounding them with seed beads, you can create a glittering effect. Use them as jewelry or combine them with tassels for shimmering interior trimmings.

Form the clay into the shape and size of bead you require. Pierce a hole through the former with a darning needle and thread it onto a wooden skewer. Before the clay former is dry, embed faceted gems evenly around its surface. Remove the gems and allow the clay to dry. Glue the gems in place around the dry former and paint the former a suitable base color to match or contrast with the seed beads you are using. Allow to dry.

Mix your seed beads with waterproof craft glue in a ratio of 2tsp of beads to 1tsp of glue. Using a popsicle stick, spread the mixture carefully over a third of the former around the gems. Make sure you do not cover the gems. Allow to dry before coating the next third, then repeat to cover the entire surface.

Remove the embellished former from the wooden skewer and use a craft knife to scrape away any glue that may have got onto the gems. (For additional help with this project refer to Encrusted beads, *page 10–11*.)

## materials

air dry modeling clay
faceted gems (not flat-backed)
waterproof craft glue
waterproof ink
seed beads

## tools

darning needle
wooden skewer
popsicle stick
paintbrush
craft knife

**Opposite:** *Faceted, inexpensive gems and colored seed beads that harmonize or contrast with each other will dazzle in the light. A versatile and eye-catching design, this produces a sparkling effect. (See left for actual bead size.)*

using
**clay**

# clay techniques

Self-hardening clay is available from craft stores in white, gray, and terra-cotta colors. It is inexpensive and easy to use.

### MAKING CLAY BEADS

**1 Cutting** To achieve a batch of evenly sized beads, roll out the clay into a sausage shape of the same diameter as the desired bead. Use a ruler and craft knife to cut the sausage neatly into equal sections.

**2 Shaping** Create a round bead by rolling a section of clay between your palms. To make a cube, squash the ball between your fingers and thumbs, as shown here.

**3 Stamping** To make flat beads, roll out the clay to the required thickness. Use aspic cutters to cut out the desired shapes or do it freehand with a craft knife.

**7 Drying** Suspend round and cubed beads on a wooden skewer when drying to prevent them from becoming distorted. Lay stamped beads on newspaper, turning them regularly.

### EMBELLISHING CLAY BEADS

**1 Painting** Using artist's acrylic paint, allow each surface to dry before painting the next. Spend some time experimenting with different color combinations.

**2 Patina** To achieve the white patina shown in the projects, apply a coat of white acrylic paint over the base color, making sure that the embossed recesses in the beads are filled with paint.

**4 Smoothing** Self-hardening clay is fibrous and therefore does not have a smooth edge when cut. To smooth it, rub its surface with a wet finger. Allow to dry for 10–20 minutes before embossing.

**5 Embossing** Experiment with different implements such as paperclips, buttons, screws, and empty pen casings to emboss interesting patterns onto your cutouts.

**6 Piercing** Using a wooden skewer, pierce a hole through the cutouts. Choose the neatest place to pierce the shape, and pierce the beads in both directions for a neater hole.

**3 Rubbing off** Rub off the surface white paint with a soft cloth. The base color will be revealed once more but the embossed recesses will retain the white paint, highlighting the pattern.

**4 Varnishing** When the paint is dry, coat the beads with matte or gloss varnish. Matte spray varnish produces the most natural effect. Keep round beads on their drying stick when varnishing.

**23**

# bedouin beads

Rolled, shaped, embossed, and inscribed, these chunky beads can be used to complement your interior decor, either on pillow corners, light pull cords, or combined with tassels for tiebacks.

Roll balls of clay between your palms to make round beads, adjusting the amount of clay you use to achieve the required size. Allow the beads to dry for 10–20 minutes to reduce surface stickiness. To make a pyramid bead, take a 1″ (2.5cm) square of clay and carefully elongate and taper the bead with a light pulling-up-and-in motion. Smooth the top with a wet finger. Allow to dry for 10–20 minutes to reduce stickiness, then press in the base of the pyramid to dome it slightly.

Decorate all the beads using tools such as empty pen casings and knitting needles until you have pleasing patterns. To make raised edges on the pyramid beads, use a wooden skewer to score a line approximately ⅛″ (2mm) in from each edge. Press the length of the stick along these scored lines to make recesses and raise the edges. Use the stick to pierce a hole through each bead. Enlarge the base hole on pyramid beads by making circular movements with the stick. Smooth around the holes and allow to dry. Coat the beads with white acrylic paint, making sure all the recesses are filled. Wipe off excess paint immediately with a soft cloth and allow to dry. Spray with matte varnish to make the beads waterproof. (For additional help with this project refer to Making clay beads/Encrusting clay beads, *pages 22–23*.)

## materials

terra-cotta self-hardening clay
white acrylic paint
matte spray varnish

## tools

embossing tools such as empty pen
   casings, knitting needles, etc.
wooden skewer
paintbrush
soft cloth

**Opposite:** *Project an authentic, ethnic look with these earthy creations. You can make them in a variety of shapes and sizes, and use them in any number of ways in your home. (See left for actual bead size.)*

# egyptian leaves

Painted in the variegated hues of green and blue to give a patina reminiscent of ancient Egypt, these engraved leaves are made from self-hardening clay. Make them into necklaces or delicate earrings.

## materials

white or gray self-hardening clay
blue, green, turquoise, and white
   acrylic paint
matte spray varnish

## tools

rolling pin and board
leaf-shaped aspic cutter
   or craft knife
needle or similar tool
wooden skewer
paintbrush
soft cloth

Roll out the clay until it is ⅛" (2mm) thick and cut or stamp out as many leaf shapes as you require. Smooth all the edges with a wet finger and allow to dry for 10–20 minutes to reduce surface stickiness. Emboss leaf veins onto the clay using a needle or similar tool. Use a wooden skewer to pierce holes in each bead. If you plan to use the beads to make a necklace, pierce sideways through the base of the stem. This will allow the leaves to lie flat against the neck when strung together. To make earring beads, pierce just below the base of the stem from front to back so that the beads face forward when hanging from the ear. Allow to dry.

Paint some of the beads with a blue base color, some green, and some turquoise. Allow to dry. Coat all the beads with white acrylic paint, then immediately rub off the surface white paint with a soft cloth. Allow to dry. If you would prefer a different color scheme, you could use terra-cotta clay with just a white patina. Spray with matte varnish to make the beads waterproof. (For additional help with this project refer to Making clay beads/Embellishing clay beads, *pages 22–23*.)

**Opposite:** *Using the colors of ancient Egypt as inspiration, these leaves, decorated in bright hues of turquoise, blue and green, are perfect for individual and stylish jewelry. (See left for actual bead size.)*

# embossed hearts

Stamped out of clay with an aspic cutter, these hearts are then embossed and allowed to dry. Once dry, they are coated with white paint that, when rubbed off, leaves a residue within the pattern.

Roll out the clay until it is ¼" (5mm) thick. Cut or stamp out as many hearts as you require. Use a wet finger to smooth the surfaces and round off the edges of the hearts. Allow to stand for 10–20 minutes to reduce surface stickiness. Emboss each heart by pressing various tools, such as knitting needles and empty pen casings, into the clay to make a pleasing pattern. Using a wooden skewer, pierce each heart from top to bottom, then allow to dry.

Once the beads are thoroughly dry, paint one side with white acrylic, making sure you fill all the embossed patterns with paint. Rub off the surface paint immediately with a soft cloth, leaving the patterns emphasized in white. Allow to dry, then repeat the process on the other side. Spray with matte varnish to make the beads waterproof. (For additional help with this project refer to Making clay beads/Embellishing clay beads, *pages 22–23*.)

## materials

---

terra-cotta self-hardening clay
white acrylic paint
matte spray varnish

## tools

---

rolling pin and board
heart-shaped aspic cutter
   or craft knife
embossing tools such as empty pen
   casings, knitting needles, etc.
wooden skewer
paintbrush
soft cloth

**Opposite:** *Put your Valentine aspic cutter to another use in making these traditional heart beads. The use of terra-cotta clay and white paint adds simplicity and warmth to this most eternal of symbols. (See above for actual bead size.)*

# birds of clay

The large bird bead would make an unusual pendant, or could be added to the end of a light pull cord. The little fledgling birds can be strung on wire along with glass beads to create flighty earrings.

Roll out the clay until it is ¼" (5mm) thick for a large bird bead and ⅛" (2mm) thick for a small bird. Cut or stamp out one halfmoon for each bird. The rest of the process is the same for both large and small birds. Create a bird's head by using a wet finger to smooth over one of the tips of the moon shape to round it off. Use a finger and thumb to pinch out a beak on the side of the head. Allow to dry for 10–20 minutes to reduce surface stickiness, then emboss the remaining pattern onto each bird. Use the tip of your cutter or knife to indent a wing shape, then add line details. Press four parallel lines for the tail. Use an empty pen casing to make a round eye, then use the tip of an old pen to dot the pupil. Repeat all the details on the opposite side, pressing lightly. Carefully pierce a hole from top to bottom using a wooden skewer. Allow to dry.

| materials |
| --- |
| white or gray self-hardening clay |
| blue, green, turquoise, and white acrylic paint |
| matte spray varnish |

| tools |
| --- |
| rolling pin and board |
| large and small halfmoon-shaped aspic cutters or craft knife |
| embossing tools such as empty pen casings, knitting needles, etc. |
| wooden skewer |
| paintbrush |
| soft cloth |

Mix up a blue-green mixture of acrylic paint as a base coat. Paint one side of each bird and allow to dry. Repeat on the opposite side. Apply a layer of white paint, making sure it fills the recesses. Wipe off the surface paint with a soft cloth immediately. Repeat on the other side. Allow to dry, then spray with matte varnish. (For additional help with this project refer to Making clay beads/Embellishing clay beads, *pages 22–23*).

**Opposite**: *For the bird-loving bead maker: In two different sizes, these embossed blue birds are fun and satisfying to make, and will add a twist to any decoration. (See left for actual bead size.)*

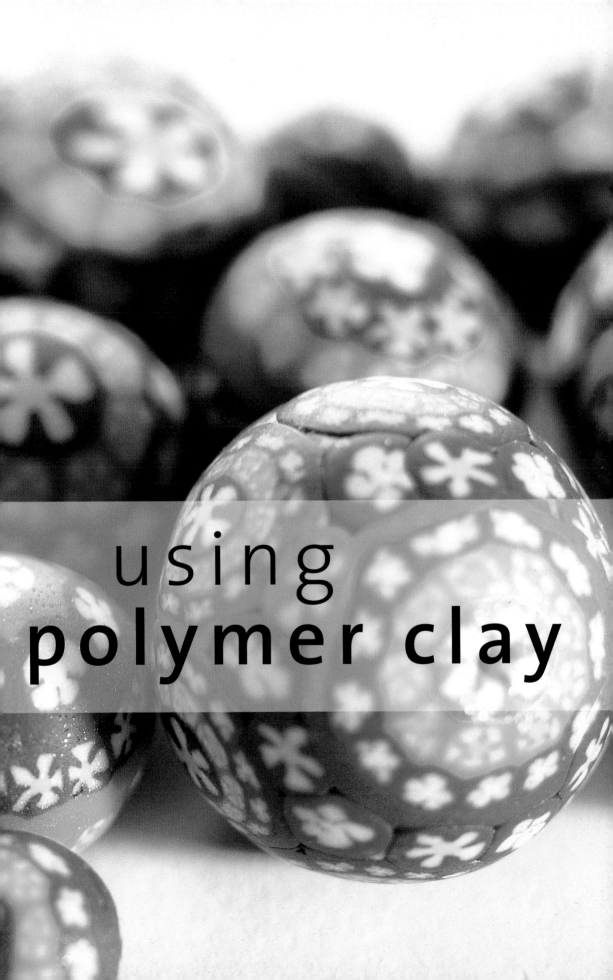

# using
# polymer clay

# general techniques

Polymer clay is available in an exciting range of colors. Knead it prior to use and bake the finished beads in an oven to harden them.

### SHAPING AND BAKING

**1 Cutting** Knead the clay, then roll out sausages using a flat board to maintain a consistent size. Cut slices from the clay using a craft knife.

**2 Forming beads** Smooth a disk of clay into a pleasing bead shape, then carefully pierce two parallel holes through the sides with a darning needle.

**3 Rolling** To add decorative shapes to the top of the base bead roll thin strands of clay, then, with a pointed wooden skewer, attach them to the bead.

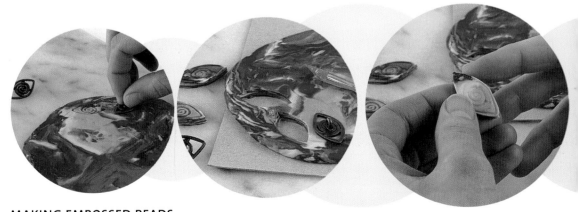

### MAKING EMBOSSED BEADS

**1 Embossing** Knead the clay (this is a good way to use up leftover scraps) and roll it out ¼″ (5mm) thick. Press the required shape into the clay.

**2 Cutting out** Place the clay on a cutting surface and cut out the embossed shape neatly with a craft knife.

**3 Smoothing** Use a finger to smooth the edges of the clay shape. Use a darning needle to pierce a hole through the bead. In this example, the hole goes through the pointed tips.

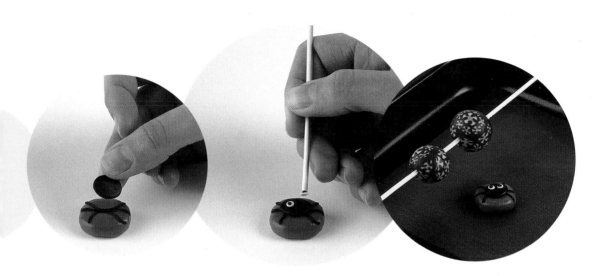

**4 Slicing** Slice sections of clay, smooth the edges and add to the base bead. Be careful not to squash the threading holes (you can keep the darning needle in place if you wish).

**5 Adding detail** Roll small balls of clay between your palms. Squash them flat and press them into the bead with a wooden skewer. You can also use the stick to etch designs.

**6 Baking** Bake the beads in an oven according to the manufacturer's instructions. Place flat beads on a baking sheet and thread round beads onto wooden skewers or wires.

**4 Coloring** Wearing a dust mask, apply metallic powder using a soft paintbrush. The powder will adhere to the tacky surface of the clay. Use several colors for a variegated finish.

**5 Blending** Shake off the excess powder, then use a soft cloth to smooth over the surface. This will blend the colors if you have used several and will ensure an even distribution of powder.

**6 Baking** Bake the beads in an oven according to the manufacturer's instructions. When dry, coat with varnish to protect the colored finish.

# millefiori techniques

This fantastic technique needs a little practice to master but is well worth the effort. You can also buy readymade millefiori canes.

### MILLEFIORI FLOWERS

**1 Rolling out** Knead the clay, then roll it into a sausage shape using a piece of Plexiglas. Roll one ½″ (1cm) diameter yellow sausage and five ⅝″ (1.5cm) diameter white sausages. All should be 2½″ (6cm) long.

**2 Forming the flower** Pinch evenly all along one side of each white sausage to create a petal shape. Arrange the white petals around the yellow center.

**3 Consolidating** Roll out and cut five red sausages of the same size as the white ones. Wedge them between the white petals and squeeze to fix the shape.

**7 Reshaping** Continue reducing the cane to the required size. You can leave it round or reshape it by pressing the cane lengthwise on a smooth surface to make faceted sides.

**8 Complex canes** Cut all the canes to the same length and pack them together as shown. Wrap a thin layer of clay around them as in step 4. Set a single thin cane aside to use later.

**9 Slicing** Roll the complex cane to consolidate it and to reduce it in size if required. Then, cut off thin slices as shown using a craft knife or sharp blade.

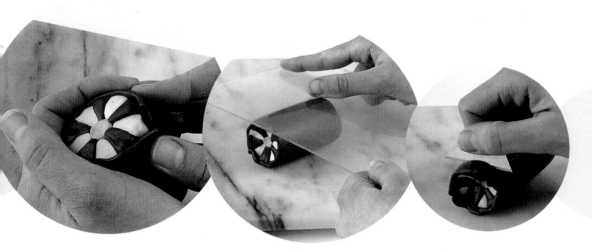

**4 Wrapping** Roll out a thin piece of red clay and wrap it around the flower. Trim to fit and smooth the edges with your thumb to seal them.

**5 Reducing** Reduce the size of the basic flower cane by rolling it gently with a piece of Plexiglas, intermittently squeezing along the cane and lightly stretching it. This will help to stop it from splitting.

**6 Trimming** As the cane lengthens, the ends will become concave. Use a craft knife or sharp blade to keep trimming them off, checking for splits in the clay before continuing the reduction process.

**10 Base beads** Use the surplus clay left over from the trimming process to make base beads (formers). Roll them between your palms to make smooth balls.

**11 Applying canes** Apply slices of the millefiori cane to the base beads. Fill gaps with slices from cane set aside in step 8. Roll the finished bead between your palms until smooth.

**12 Piercing and baking** Use a darning needle to pierce a hole through the bead, first from one side and then the other. Bake in an oven according to the manufacturer's instructions.

# dabbling ducks

These ducks are easier to make than you might think. The initial cane is large and manageable. The trick is in the stretching and rolling, to reduce the original duck into miniature ducklings.

## materials

1 block each of white, light blue, and navy blue polymer clay

¼ block of yellow polymer clay

## tools

piece of Plexiglas
craft knife or sharp blade
wooden skewer
darning needle
baking sheet

Knead the white and light blue clay. Use a piece of Plexiglas to roll out a 1" (2.5cm) diameter, 1½" (3cm) long sausage of white clay. Cut in half lengthwise to create two half cylinders. Cut one of these in half again so that you have two quarter cylinders. Discard one quarter. Use the half cylinder to make the duck's body. Place your thumbs in the middle and gently pull both long edges upward with your fingers to create a crescent shape. Roll the quarter cylinder into a sausage shape to make the duck's head. Cut this sausage in half lengthwise and press a wooden skewer along the flat side of both pieces. The stick should form a central core when you put the two halves back together. Remove the stick, roll a thin sausage of light blue clay, placing it along the central core, and sandwich the two halves of white clay back together. The light blue clay forms the duck's eye. Cut a 1½" (3cm) long triangular wedge from the corner of a block of yellow clay and place it against the duck's head to form a beak. Position the head against the body.

Roll a fat 1½" (3cm) long sausage of light blue clay. Place the duck against one end and use a needle to inscribe the outline of the duck shape onto the clay. Cut away all the light blue clay surrounding the inscribed shape in wedge-shaped portions. As you do so, pack these wedges around the duck cane in the correct positions. Finish the duck by wrapping it in a layer of light blue and then navy blue clay. Reduce the cane to the required size, slice it into ¼" (5mm) thick beads, pierce holes with a needle, and bake to harden. (For additional help with this project refer to Millefiori techniques, *pages 36–37.*)

**Opposite**: *A truly innovative and fun bead, these pretty ducks are made with different-colored blocks of polymer clay. Children will love them. (See left for actual bead size.)*

# millefiori magic

Once you've got the knack of creating polymer clay canes, the magic of millefiori will become addictive. Watching the image in a large cane being reduced into miraculous miniatures is delightful.

Start by kneading all of the clay, then use Plexiglas to roll each block of white clay into a long, wide sausage shape. Divide each sausage into five equal portions. Roll the yellow clay into a sausage that is a bit thinner than the white ones and cut into three sections equal in length to the white ones. Make three white flowers with yellow centers.

Roll a block of red clay into a sausage equal in length to the flowers. Cut the red sausage into wedge-shaped sections. Pack the wedges between the petals of one of the flowers, shaping the wedges as required to accommodate the petal shapes. Roll out the remaining half block of red clay to a thin layer and wrap it around the flower. Repeat this process with blue clay for the second flower and green clay for the third flower. Roll the three flower canes to reduce them to the required size.

When making a complex cane, first choose your color combination. For example, use a single red flower as the center of the complex cane, then surround it by green flowers and then blue ones. To make the finished bead, follow steps 10, 11, and 12 of the techniques (*pages 36–37*).

| materials |
| --- |
| 3 blocks of white polymer clay |
| ¾ block of yellow polymer clay |
| 1½ blocks each of red, blue, and green polymer clay |

| tools |
| --- |
| piece of Plexiglas |
| craft knife or sharp blade |
| darning needle |

**Opposite:** *Colorful and instantly recognizable with their amazingly intricate designs, millefiori beads are very satisfying to craft. (See left for actual bead size.)*

# multicolored bugs

Use vibrant-colored polymer clay to create these beads. The distinct markings of a ladybug are a good starting point, then use your imagination to make a menagerie of creepy crawlies.

## materials

¼ block each of lime green, leaf green, turquoise, and dark green polymer clay

scraps of polymer clay in vivid colors

waterproof craft glue

## tools

craft knife

darning needle

baking sheet

Start by kneading and rolling the quarter blocks of clay into four 1" (2.5cm) diameter sausages. Cut them into ¼" (5mm) thick beads. Use a finger to smooth around the edges of the beads, then make parallel holes ½" (1cm) apart through the sides of the beads with a darning needle.

For the legs, roll slithers of different-colored clays and cut them into sections long enough to span the beads and position three pieces across each bead. Roll and cut ½" (1cm) diameter disks in different-colored clays and squeeze them into flattened oval shapes. Trim off the top quarter of each disk with a craft knife. The top quarter forms the bug's head and the larger portion forms the body. Pair up heads and bodies in different colors.

Using the side of a darning needle, press a line down the back for the wings. Use the blunt end of the needle to emboss the clay where the spots and eyes should go. Roll thin sausages of clay and cut off tiny amounts to form into balls. Press each ball into a recessed spot, using different colors for the bodies and eyes. Glue the head and body into position over the legs. Make a small ball for each foot and press in place on the end of each leg. Check that the holes are still open with the darning needle, then bake according to the manufacturer's instructions. (For additional help with this project refer to shaping and baking, *pages 34–35*.)

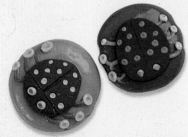

**Opposite:** *These lively ladybugs are easy and fun to make and can be as vivid as you like. Pair the heads and bodies in different shades and string onto an elastic cord for a child's bracelet. (See left for actual bead size.)*

# phosphorescent fish

Silver blue, copper, and purple metallic powders have been applied to these polymer clay fish, followed by layers of varnish for a durable finish. Add a diamanté to put a sparkle in their eyes.

## materials

polymer clay

metallic powders in various colors

matte spray varnish

waterproof craft glue

diamantés

## tools

thin cardboard

pencil

craft knife

rolling pin and board

knitting needle and safety pin

soft brush and soft cloth

baking sheet

Draw the outline of a fish approximately 1½" (3.5cm) long and ½" (1.5cm) wide on some thin cardboard and cut out to form a template. Start by kneading the clay. Roll it out flat until it is ¼" (5mm) thick. Place the template onto the clay and lightly draw around it with the point of a knitting needle. Repeat until you have enough fish. Use a craft knife to cut out each fish shape. Rub your thumb along the edges to smooth them. Press the blunt end of the knitting needle into the clay to make the eye socket on one side of each fish. Emboss lines into the clay for the tail and mouth with the pointed end of a safety pin, then use the rounded end to create scallop shapes for the scales. Repeat on the other side.

Use a soft brush to apply metallic powder to each fish, blending the different colors with a soft cloth. Do this to both sides, then bake in an oven according to the manufacturer's instructions. Allow to cool. Apply three coats of varnish one side at a time, allowing each coat to dry before applying the next. As a final touch, glue a diamanté into the eye socket on each side of the fish. (For additional help with this project refer to Making embossed beads, *pages 34–35.*)

**Opposite**: *Create the beguiling effect of shimmering, tropical fish by using cool, metallic shades, and have fun embossing the scales with the rounded end of a safety pin. (See left for actual bead size.)*

using
**felt**

# felt techniques

All you need to create these tactile beads is some fleece (unspun yarn) and hot, soapy water. They are very easy and satisfying to make.

### MAKING FELT BEADS

**1 Winding** Tie a knot at the end of the fleece and wrap it around to form a tight, even ball. Make it about twice as big as your intended bead because it will shrink considerably.

**2 Dipping** Dip the ball into hot, soapy water. Squeeze it to make sure that the water penetrates right to the heart of the bead.

### EMBELLISHING FELT BEADS

**Stripes** Press a pin into opposite sides of the bead. These will allow you to hold the bead without obstructing the decoration. Using fabric dye pens, slowly revolve the bead against the pen to make a stripe.

**Spots** Press pins to the bead as before. Use fabric dye pens to draw spots all over the bead. It is best to map out the spots with tiny, faint dots at first, and when you have a suitable configuration, enlarge them into the required size spots.

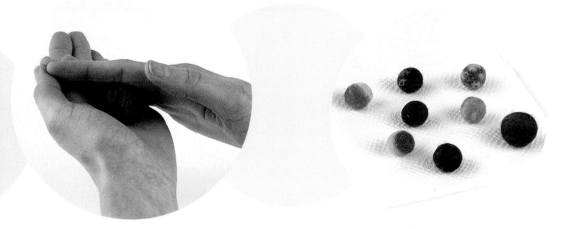

**3 Rolling** Roll the bead between your palms, gently at first but increasing the pressure as the fibers begin to mat together. Repeat the dipping and rolling process until you achieve the required size. Rinse out the soap.

**4 Drying** Lay out the beads on paper towels or another absorbent material. Allow to dry, turning the beads regularly. They will take quite a while to dry thoroughly. To speed up the process, put them in a linen closet or near a radiator.

**Bugle beads** Use transparent nylon thread and a beading needle to stitch bugle beads onto the felt base bead. Position randomly and at different angles to add liveliness. Stitch securely and make sure the initial and final knots in the thread are tight.

**Seed beads** Thread lots of seed beads onto some transparent nylon thread. Wrap the beaded thread around the felt base bead, attaching it to the felt with a few small stitches to hold the seed beads securely in place.

# psychedelic marbles

Dyed fleece in fresh, tangy colors has been felted together to produce these soft, light beads. They are easy to make and ideal for transforming into jewelry or interior trimmings.

Tie a knot at the end of a length of fleece, then wrap the fleece around the knot to build up a ball. Use layers of different colors until you get a pleasing mixture. Try to keep the shape even by winding in different directions until you have a ball approximately twice the size of your intended bead. Dip the bead into a bowl of hot, soapy water, squeezing it to make sure the water has penetrated it fully. Roll the bead between the palms of your hands and repeat the dipping and rolling process several times. As the fibers begin to melt, increase the pressure in your palms until you have reached a suitable size. Rinse out the soap and lay the finished beads on a paper towel or another absorbent material. Allow them to dry, remembering to turn regularly.

The beads are easy to string together. All you have to do is stitch through the middle of each bead with a needle and thread. A necklace of felt beads in graduated sizes and different colors looks good. These beads can also be washed in warm, soapy water. (For additional help with this project refer to Making felt beads, *pages 48–49.*)

| materials |
| --- |
| fleece in a variety of vivid colors, such as lime green, turquoise, pink, purple, yellow, and orange |

| tools |
| --- |
| bowl of hot, soapy water paper towels |

**Opposite:** *Tactile and versatile, these felt beads in brightly contrasting colors can be used in many different designs. Remember that the bead will shrink during the creative process. (See left for actual bead size.)*

# spotted & striped

These large, compacted beads definitely have the squeeze factor.
The base beads were made in pink and cream, and then spots and
stripes of cheerful colors were added using fabric dye pens.

---

## materials

cream and pink fleece
orange, pink, and lime green fabric
  dye pens

## tools

bowl of hot, soapy water
paper towels
pins

---

Tie a knot at the end of a length of cream fleece,
then wrap the fleece around the knot to build up a
ball about twice the size of your intended bead.
Repeat with the pink fleece. Dip the beads into a
bowl of hot, soapy water, squeezing them to make
sure the water has penetrated fully throughout.
Roll the beads between the palms of your hands
and repeat the dipping and rolling process until
they reach the required size. You should roll and
squeeze these beads more than usual so that their
surface is well-compacted and suitable for drawing
on. A good way to test whether the beads have
shrunk sufficiently is to throw them hard on a
tabletop. They will bounce when fully felted. Rinse out all the soap thoroughly and lay the
finished beads on a paper towel or similar absorbent material. Allow them to dry, turning
regularly.

Press pins into opposite sides of the beads and use these to hold the beads while you draw
vibrant lines or spots over their surfaces with fabric dye pens in different colors. (For additional
help with this project refer to Making felt beads/Embellishing felt beads, *pages 48–49*.)

**Opposite:** *There are many ways of embellishing felt
beads, and these spots and stripes are particularly effective.
Let your imagination run wild and have fun with fabric
dye pens of all colors. (See left for actual bead size.)*

# disco divas

The rich, purple felt and the cool, angular silver beads make a dynamic combination. These beads make eye-catching jewelry that glints in the light.

Tie a knot at the end of a length of purple fleece, then wrap the fleece around the knot. When the ball of fleece is twice the size of your intended bead, dip it into a bowl of hot, soapy water. Squeeze, dip, and roll the beads between the palms of your hands until they reach the required size. Rinse out all the soap, lay the finished beads on a paper towel, and allow to dry, turning regularly.

Thread a beading needle with transparent nylon thread. Tie a knot in the end of the thread and stitch into the felt bead. Thread a bugle bead onto the needle and take another stitch. Continue to stitch on beads at different angles until the whole bead is covered. Be sure that the knots in the nylon thread are secure.

You could make smaller beads using the same recipe to use as earrings. The whole bead can be used for dangling earrings, or they can be cut in half with a craft knife (before the beads are sewn on), dipped in waterproof craft glue, and an appropriate earring finding glued onto them. (For additional help with this project refer to Making felt beads/Embellishing felt beads, *pages 48–49.*)

## materials

-----

purple fleece
silver bugle beads
transparent nylon thread

## tools

-----

bowl of hot, soapy water
paper towels
beading needle

**Opposite**: *These purple felt and silver beads make funky and fashionable ornaments—whether as original jewelry or as Christmas tree decorations with a difference. (See left for actual bead size.)*

using **natural**
**materials**

# preparing naturals

## WORKING WITH SEEDS

**1 Threading** Wash the seeds and remove any pith. Lay out the seeds on some newspaper and allow to dry. Pierce the dried seeds with a darning needle and string them onto thread.

**2 Forming a flower** Roll a small bead of self-hardening clay, squash it flat, then press five seeds into the clay bead at their most pointed ends and arrange as petals.

**2 Attaching** There are many ways to attach shells. An easy method is to use stranded floss (embroidery thread) to stitch through the holes in the shell and around a piece of cord several times. Tie the ends of the floss together inside the shell where it will be concealed. Secure with glue.

## WORKING WITH SLATE

**1 Sanding** Slate is a soft stone and is therefore easy to sand smooth using a sanding sponge. You can sometimes find pieces of slate on beaches, and very often their shapes require no beautification.

**3 Gluing petals** Remove the seeds and allow the clay bead to dry. Glue the petals into place and allow to dry. Paint with nail varnish for a more durable and glossy finish.

## WORKING WITH SHELLS
**1 Drilling** Position the part of the shell that is to be drilled against a piece of wood. Support the shell with a piece of modeling clay. Drill steadily without too much pressure to prevent breakage.

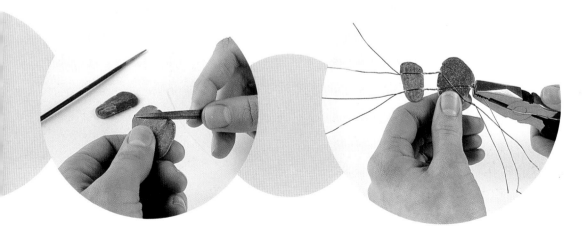

**2 Filing** File pairs of notches at the top and bottom of each piece of slate with a needle file. You can then use these notches to attach pieces of slate together. If you prefer, you can drill holes through slate in the same way as shells; again, do not apply too much pressure.

**3 Binding** Use two pairs of wires, one pair for the top set of notches and the other for the bottom notches. Slot the pieces of slate between the paired wires and use pliers to twist the wire into the notches to hold the stones securely.

# paper techniques

Using recycled paper is one of the cheapest and most enjoyable ways of making beads. Once dry, these beads are hard and durable.

**PAPIER-MÂCHÉ BEADS**

**1 Soaking** Tear newspaper into small pieces and place them in a heatproof bowl. Cover with boiling water and allow to soak for three hours.

**2 Blending** Using an electric hand blender or whisk, blend the paper to a smooth pulp (avoid overworking your blender).

**3 Draining** Place the blended pulp into a strainer and squeeze out the excess water by pressing a spoon all over the pulp.

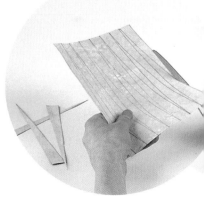

**7 Painting a base** Decide on a base color. Using a soft paintbrush and leaving the bead on the wooden skewer, apply artist's acrylic paint. Allow to dry.

**8 Decorating** You can decorate the beads by painting a pattern on them with acrylic paint or permanent marker pens. Spray the finished beads with matte or gloss varnish.

**ROLLED PAPER BEADS**

**1 Cutting** The eventual size and shape of your bead depends on the size of the triangle that you cut. Use a pencil to mark out opposing triangles on your chosen paper and cut out.

**4 Binding** Mix equal quantities of powdered wallpaper paste and spackle (decorator's filler). Blend this into the paper pulp until you have achieved a clay-like consistency.

**5 Shaping** Roll a piece of the mixture between your palms to make a bead. Pierce with a darning needle from both sides, then thread onto a wooden skewer and allow to dry.

**6 Sanding** The beads will take several days to dry thoroughly and you may find that they become pitted. Use fine-grit sandpaper to smooth the surface and remove imperfections.

**2 Rolling** Starting at the triangle base, roll the paper around a wooden skewer with the pattern outside. Spread glue over the last 1″ (2.5cm) of the triangle tip. Roll up and allow to dry.

**PAPER FLOWERS**
**1 Scrunching** Spread wallpaper paste over a strip of tissue paper and fold in half lengthwise. Wind the strip into a spiral, squeezing the base as you go to create a flower effect.

**2 Threading** Once the flowers are dry, use a sharp darning needle to pierce a hole through the base of each flower. Thread the flowers onto a length of elastic or other suitable material.

# seashore treasures

Shells are natural beads, from the simple cockle to the mother of
pearl, and they can easily be turned into jewelry. These rainbow
cockles, sewn onto a rough cotton cord, make an unusual necklace.

Referring to Working with shells (*pages 58–59*), drill
holes in the noses of the cockleshells large enough
to accommodate the stranded floss you are using.
Fold the cotton cord in half and position the
largest shell at the halfway point. Arrange the
remaining shells in diminishing sizes along both
ends of the cord. Check that they span out as
much as you require. Thread a darning needle with
embroidery floss and tie a knot 1" (2.5cm) from
the end. Stitch through the center of the cord at
the halfway mark to anchor the floss, then
overstitch around the cord and through the central
shell. Tie the ends of the floss together securely
inside the shell where they will be hidden, gluing
them in place if necessary. Repeat the process until
all the shells are in position.

Try on the necklace, tying the cord at the back
of the neck. The ends will hang down your back. If you like, you could finish off the ends like
tassels by gluing each one tight inside a whelk shell. Alternately, you may prefer to use a
conventional necklace clasp to hold the cord.

## materials

rainbow cockleshells in
   diminishing sizes
stranded floss (embroidery thread)
cotton cord
glue (if necessary)
2 whelk shells or a conventional
   necklace clasp (optional)

## tools

hobby drill and piece of wood
scrap of modeling clay
darning needle

**Opposite:** *Shells are one of the most beautiful natural
resources for jewelry and interior decoration and, in
addition, require very little adornment. Be careful not to
crack the shell when drilling. (See left for actual bead size.)*

# elegant slates

Smooth, seaworn slate and hard, linear wire make a terrific combination for jewelry. The white plastic-coated wire mimics the structural lines that can often be found in this type of stone.

## materials

pieces of seaworn slate
white plastic-coated copper wire
frosted glass beads
clasp

## tools

chalk
sanding sponge
needle file
wire cutters
pliers

Arrange the pieces of slate into a necklace shape—it usually looks best if the largest piece is positioned centrally. With chalk, mark any places where you need to alter the shape of the stones or make them smaller. One by one, sand away any unwanted parts or form new shapes, making sure all the edges are smooth.

Once all the finished stones are back in your arrangement, mark where the connecting wires need to run (this depends on the shape of the stones). In this example, the wire runs along the necklace a third of the way down the stones, with occasional random excursions around the bottom. File pairs of grooves on each stone deep enough to accommodate the wire at the marked positions.

Cut two 1.5m lengths of wire. Allowing 1' (30cm) excess at the end, place the wires on either side of the first stone. Use pliers to twist the wires together right into the grooves to hold the stones securely. Thread on a frosted glass bead between each stone until all stones are held firmly in place. Complete the necklaces with frosted beads and a clasp. (For additional help with this project refer to Working with slate, *pages 58–59*.)

*Opposite: The natural look of slate—here made into a striking necklace with frosted glass beads—is sensational. Make sure all the edges are smoothed off, in order to show off the stone at its best. (See left for actual bead size.)*

# flower power

Dried pips and seeds make a natural durable bead that can be dyed, varnished, painted, or plain. Here, nail polish gives these petals their gloss. Use single flowers or link them together.

## materials

melon, pumpkin, squash, or other
   types of seed
white self-hardening clay
yellow acrylic paint
colored nail polish
strong glue
jump rings

## tools

empty pen casing
paintbrush
newspaper
darning needle

Wash and clean the seeds. When they are dry, roll small balls of clay between the palms of your hands. Press the balls to flatten them, then push the most pointed ends of the seeds into the clay to make flower petals. Emboss circles into the clay with an empty pen casing. Remove all the seed petals and allow the clay centers to dry. Then paint them with yellow acrylic paint, and paint the seeds with colored nail polish. Allow to dry. Glue the seeds into position around the clay centers and leave to set.

The flowers can be linked together to form a necklace or bracelet using three jump rings between each flower or hung on an earring by one jump ring. Place the petals to be pierced against some folded newspaper. Push a darning needle through to make a hole close enough to the tip of the petal to accommodate a jump ring. (For additional help with this project refer to Working with seeds, *pages 58–59.*)

**Opposite**: *Pips and seeds are a pretty form of decoration and can be arranged in a number of different ways for various, attractive effects. There are many types of seed you could use. (See left for actual bead size.)*

# safari beads

Zebra stripes and leopard spots combine with other animal markings to create these wild papier-mâché beads. Intermingle them on bracelets and necklaces for dynamic and exciting jewelry.

Referring to Papier-mâché beads (*pages 60–61*), prepare the newspaper pulp and form the mixture into the required size beads. To make a safari necklace, form a large central bead about 1" (2.5cm) in diameter and six pairs of beads to go on either side of the central bead, gradually decreasing in size down to ¼" (5mm). Make pea-size beads for the rest of the necklace. Pierce holes in the beads with a darning needle, then thread them onto wooden skewers and allow to dry. Sand the dry beads if necessary, then paint them with a suitable base coat color and allow to dry.

Using a medium- and thin-tipped black marker pen, draw a pattern of large, irregular hexagonal spots and stripes on the beads. Spread them randomly over the surface. Fill in the space around them or within them using tan-colored pens. Varnish to prevent the paint from chipping (test first to check the reaction of the paint and pens). (For additional help with this project refer to Papier-mâché beads, pages 60–61.)

## materials

newspaper
wallpaper paste and spackle
 (decorator's filler)
acrylic paint for base coat
thin- and medium-tipped permanent
 marker pens in black and tan
thick gloss varnish

## tools

heatproof bowl and electric hand
 blender or whisk
strainer and spoon
darning needle and kabob (kebab)
 sticks
fine-grit sandpaper (if necessary)
brushes for paint and varnish

**Opposite**: *Go wild with these safari beads in black and tan. Using papier mâché to create the bead, create your own patterns inspired by the African veld with colored marker pens. (See left for actual bead size.)*

# wrap & roll

Whether you use origami paper or scraps of wallpaper, these beads are simple and elegant. To prolong their life, apply several coats of varnish, first checking the varnish does not cause the colors to run.

## materials

7½" (20cm) squares of origami or
   other type of decorative paper
glue
thick varnish (optional)

## tools

pencil
ruler
craft knife or scissors
kabob (kebab) stick
applicators for glue and varnish

To make the large beads pictured opposite, use a pencil and ruler to mark 1½" (3cm) intervals along one side of a square of paper. Mark a ¾" (2cm) margin at either end of the opposite side of the paper. Mark 1½" (3cm) intervals along the edge between the two margins. Connect the marked points across the page with a ruler so that you have three complete triangular shapes in the center and two half shapes at either end.

Cut out all of these. Sweep the side of the ruler across each complete triangular shape to curl the paper. One by one, roll these triangles around a wooden skewer, working from their base upward. Apply glue to the last 1" (2.5cm) at the tip of the triangle and wrap it around the bead to hold the paper in place. Allow the beads to dry. You can simply alter the dimensions of the triangles to make smaller beads.

The beads formed from complete triangles of paper are suitable for making necklaces. You can roll up the two extra half triangles from the sides of each square of paper to make cone shapes for matching dangling earrings.

To prolong the life of your beads, you can paint them with varnish (but remember to do a test strip first in order to check that the colors will not run). (For additional help with this project refer to Rolled paper beads, *pages 60–61*.)

**Opposite**: *Instead of throwing away scraps of your favorite wallpaper, try this easy, wrap and roll technique. The resulting bead can be used to create jewelry with smooth, stylish lines. (See left for actual bead size.)*

# floral fiesta

Brightly colored tissue paper has been sculpted into flowers and
leaves to make these fun paper beads. Thread them onto colored
elastic to make lively garlands for your head, neck, or wrist.

Cut a 4" x 6" (10cm x 15cm) strip of tissue paper for each flower in the colors of your choice.
Spread wallpaper paste over each strip and fold them in half lengthwise. Work carefully because
the damp paper disintegrates easily. Wind the strip into a crinkly spiral, squeezing the base to
form the base of the flower petals. Allow to dry.

Cut out leaf shapes from white cardstock (card).
Each leaf should be approximately 1½" (3cm) long
and ½" (1cm) wide. Then cut 2" x 2½" (5cm x 6cm)
strips of green tissue. Coat the green tissue with
wallpaper paste and wrap each piece around a leaf,
scrunching the paper in places to follow the shape
of the leaf. Allow to dry.

Paint the dried flowers and leaves with liberal
coats of gloss varnish, allowing each layer to dry
before applying the next. The flowers and leaves
should be rigid when finished. Use a darning
needle to pierce holes in the base of the flowers
and leaves, then thread them onto elastic in a
pleasing and creative arrangement. (For additional
help with this project refer to Paper flowers, *pages
60–61.*)

## materials

tissue paper in green and floral colors
wallpaper paste
thin white cardstock (card)
thick gloss varnish

## tools

scissors or craft knife
brushes for applying wallpaper paste
   and varnish
darning needle

**Opposite:** *For those who love flowers, these delicate
tissue petals, hardened with glossy varnish, make beautiful
floral arrangements and garlands in a variety of colors.
(See left for actual bead size.)*

using
aromatics

# aromatic techniques

Create wonderful perfumed jewelry using gums, spices, and flower petals. The results are as pleasing for the nose as they are for the eye.

**THREADING AROMATICS**

**1 Heating the needle** When making holes in small or soft items such as incense, pierce them with a hot needle. Place the tip of a sewing needle into a candle flame until it becomes red hot (take care not to burn your fingers).

**2 Piercing** Wipe the needle clean of soot with a cloth, then pierce or melt a hole through the incense using the needle.

**5 Drilling difficult shapes** Take care with brittle spices, such as star anise. Decide which way around you want the star to hang. Place the top point sideways against a piece of wood and drill very carefully through the side of the point.

**6 Threading** Soak spices (such as cloves) in water overnight so that they become soft and pliable. Use a sewing needle with a double length of thread to string as required.

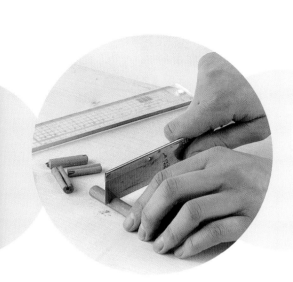

**3 Sawing** When selecting long shapes for threading, saw them to the desired length. For cinnamon sticks choose ones that are compact and not too flaky. Mark out regular intervals using a ruler. Saw from the bridge on the back of the sticks.

**4 Drilling** Secure round objects in a pair of pliers with the top uppermost. Stretch a strong rubber band around the plier handles to keep them secure. With the drill bit, press a dent into the top of the object, then slowly drill through.

## FLOWERS
**1 Tearing petals** Remove the hard white attachment tip from the petals, then tear them into small pieces.

**2 Forming beads** When making rose petal beads, keep some petals aside. These can be used to coat the bead to give a more pleasing finish.

# arabian nights

When you wear a necklace of these spicy beads, your body heat will intensify the exotic aroma. The beads combine fragrant rosewater and a mixture of pungent spices.

## materials

1½ tbsp powdered orrisroot

1½ tbsp basil

1 tbsp each of powdered gum benzoin, cinnamon, and mace

½ tsp ground cloves

½ tsp freshly grated nutmeg

a few drops each of cedarwood, myrrh, and sandalwood essential oils

1 tsp gum tragacanth powder

3–4 tbsp triple-strength rosewater

whole cardamom pods

thread

## tools

2 mixing bowls

darning needle

Mix all the dry herbs and spices together in a large bowl. Stir in the essential oils gradually. In a separate bowl, mix together the gum tragacanth and rosewater. Stir this into the first mixture to form a dough. Add more rosewater if the dough is too dry, then pinch off small amounts and roll into pea-size beads. If the beads are too sticky, roll them in a mixture of dry spices. Pierce each bead using a darning needle and allow to dry until hard.

Use a darning needle and a double length of thread to string up the beads, alternating each spicy bead with three cardamom pods.

**Opposite:** *A stimulating mix of spices, rosewater and essential oils combines to form these exotically scented beads, which are rewarding to make. The fusion of these natural fragrances is dynamic yet subtle.*

# rose petal beads

Traditionally, rose petal beads were strung onto rosaries, infusing prayer with a sweet fragrance. These delicate beads can be used for that purpose, for jewelry, or to scent your clothes.

Referring to Flowers (*page 77*), remove the white tip of each petal and tear into small pieces. Keep some of the smaller petals aside. If you have any miniature roses use the petals from these. (See Flowers technique on *page 77.*)

To each cup of torn rose petals add ½ tsp powdered arris root and 2 tbsp acacia powder adding a little rosewater at a time. Mix together to make a stiff paste and place in a double boiler over a medium heat, until you begin to see the oils seep out. Mix with your wooden spoon to make a dough.

Put a pea-sized amount into the center of one of the small petals that you have put aside. Rub a few drops of rose oil into the palms of your hands, wrap the petal around the dough, and roll between your palms. Allow to dry on wax paper (greaseproof paper). Before it is completely dry pierce it with a darning needle or leave until completely dry, then drill a hole through the center. Repeat until all the mixture is used up.

## materials

torn rose petals
½ tsp powdered orrisroot
acacia powder (also known as
    Gum Arabic)
drops of rose oil (or unscented
    vegetable oil)
triple-strength rosewater

## tools

double boiler
wooden spoon
darning needle
wax paper (greaseproof paper)

**Opposite:** *For centuries, rose petals have been used in arts and crafts. The delicate scent of these beads can be used in modern interiors as well as in the creation of unique, timeless jewelry. (See left for actual bead size.)*

# spice bazaar

Ward off winter blues with this aromatic necklace. Thread together cloves, allspice, star anise, and nutmeg to make an intoxicating combination of irresistible fragrances.

Refer to the Aromatic techniques on (*pages 76–77*) when making this necklace. Start by soaking the cloves and allspice in water overnight. Drill holes in the nutmegs and star anise. With a sewing needle and double length of brown thread, string up your necklace, using the best star anise as the centerpiece. Push the needle through the wet cloves just below the head and string them in small groups interspersed with allspice approximately every 2½" (6cm). Thread on a nutmeg or star anise at attractive intervals until your necklace is long enough to go comfortably over your head to your preferred length. Tie the ends securely and hide the knot between the cloves.

## materials

whole cloves, allspice, nutmegs,
   and star anise
brown thread

## tools

bowl
hobby drill and piece of wood
pliers and rubber band
sewing needle

**Opposite:** *Cloves are a festive, traditional spice and, when combined with other spices as in this aromatic and exotic arrangement, can make all occasions special. (See left for actual bead size.)*

# balmy beads

Cardamom pods, rosebuds, cinnamon sticks, and gums make up this intricate and fragrant necklace. The scent will last for several months and can be revived by rubbing scented oil into the beads.

## materials

large pieces of incense in amber, frankincense, and myrrh
cinnamon sticks
rosebuds
clear spray varnish
whole cardamom pods
thread

## tools

candle
sewing needle
small craft saw
hobby drill and piece of wood

Refer to the Aromatic techniques on (*pages 76–77*) when making this necklace. Start by making holes through the pieces of incense with a red-hot needle, making sure you wipe the soot off before piercing them. Saw the cinnamon sticks into ¾" (2cm) sections and carefully drill holes through their centers. Spray each rosebud with a layer of clear varnish and allow to dry. Using a sewing needle with a double length of thread, string up the cardamom pods and pieces of incense in groups of three, interspersing each group with a piece of cinnamon stick or a rosebud. Make a long, leisurely necklace in a pleasing arrangement, tying the ends of the thread together when it is long enough to go over your head comfortably.

**Opposite:** *The delicious aroma of this fine piece of jewelry has its base in amber, frankincense and myrrh incense. Rosebuds add both a romantic touch and a subtle fragrance.*

using
plastic

# plastic techniques

"Friendly Plastic" is a type of plastic that can be cut with scissors and baked in an oven to meld the pieces together.

### ASSEMBLING BEADS

**1 Cutting** Friendly Plastic comes in flat sheets in a wide range of colors. Cut the shapes you require from the sheets using a sharp pair of scissors.

**2 Arranging** Place the pieces on a nonstick baking parchment on a baking sheet. Using tweezers, position the elements together, making sure they all touch.

### LAYERING

**1 Cutting** Use a pair of sharp scissors to cut the shapes you plan to layer in diminishing sizes. Cut other shapes to be added to the sides of the bead.

**2 Making the base** Place the largest shape on a piece of nonstick baking parchment on a baking sheet. Position the medium-size piece on top. Bake according to the manufacturer's instructions so that the two shapes meld together.

**3 Baking** Bake in an oven according to the manufacturer's instructions. Check that all the elements have melded together. If not, push them together again and repeat the baking process.

**4 Applying contrasting materials** Add other materials (such as sequins) to the bead once it has cooled. Scratch with a needle the surfaces to be adhered, and fix in place with craft glue.

**3 Adding** Add elements to the side and top of the bead and bake once again to meld the pieces. Hold a needle in the flame of a candle until it is red hot, wipe off the soot, and pierce holes in appropriate positions for jump rings.

**4 Oblong linking beads** Make oblong beads to intersperse between more elaborate beads. Use tweezers to position random slivers of different colored plastic on top or, alternately, a narrow oblong of plastic. Bake as before and pierce each end with a red-hot needle.

# heart art

These sassy hearts in hot, vibrant colors can be made into a charm bracelet or necklace. Hung from silver chains or black leather thongs, they make jewelry that is light, fun, and inexpensive.

## materials

gold, red, and pink Friendly
   Plastic strips

## tools

scissors
nonstick baking parchment and
   baking sheet
tweezers
candle
darning needle

Use sharp scissors to cut ½" (1cm) squares of plastic in different colors. Cut heart shapes of a similar size to the squares in different colors. Cut more heart shapes but make them slightly smaller, then cut little circles of plastic. Place the squares and large hearts on some nonstick baking parchment on a baking sheet. Use tweezers to position some of the small hearts on top of the large hearts and some on top of the squares. Decorate the remaining large hearts with the circles. Bake according to the manufacturer's instructions. Check that all parts are melded together. If they are not, push the pieces together more closely and repeat the baking process. Heat a darning needle in the flame of a candle until it is red hot. Wipe off the soot and pierce a hole through the top of each heart bead.

**Opposite:** *Wear your heart on a sleeve and make a flamboyant charm bracelet with a difference. When baked, Friendly Plastic melds different shapes together for vivid and versatile designs.*

# little angels

To ensure that these guardian angels always travel with you, attach jump rings through their halos and suspend them from a chain. They are perfect for a child's necklace or charm bracelet.

## materials

silver, metallic blue, metallic purple, and flesh color Friendly Plastic strips
sequins
strong glue (optional)

## tools

scissors
tweezers
nonstick baking parchment and baking sheet
candle
darning needle

Cut out all the elements—a triangle for the dress, two triangles for the wings, two oblongs for the legs, and a circle for the head—with a pair of sharp scissors. Using tweezers, place the dress on a piece of nonstick baking parchment on a baking sheet. Position the head, wings, and legs. Put the baking sheet in an oven and bake according to the manufacturer's instructions. Check that all the elements have melded together. If they have not, push them together with tweezers and rebake.

The sequin halo can be attached either by melding it into the back of the head while the angel is still soft from the oven or gluing it on later (in which case you need to scratch both surfaces with a needle prior to gluing). Heat a darning needle in the flame of a candle until the tip is red-hot. Wipe off the soot, then melt a hole in the top of the halo large enough to insert a jump ring. These can hang from earrings or in a row along a chain. (For additional help with this project refer to Assembling beads, *pages 88–89*.)

**Opposite:** *These little angels are irresistible and very easy to make. The combination of silver, metallic-colored Friendly Plastic strips and sequins for ornamentation guarantee a heavenly result. (See left for actual bead size.)*

# Inca totems

Link together these totems to make a stunning necklace and earrings. These beads are based on the Inca style, but the metallic and pearlized finish makes them unmistakably modern.

Cut three squares in diminishing sizes—the largest square should measure ½"(1cm). Cut six triangles measuring ¼" (5mm) at the base from different colored plastic for each bead. Place the largest squares onto some nonstick baking parchment on a baking sheet. Use tweezers to position the medium squares in the center of the large squares and bake according to the manufacturer's instructions until they are melded together. Put the smallest squares on top of the other two and place two triangles at the top and two at the bottom of each square bead, making sure all the pieces are in contact. Repeat the baking process and allow to cool.

Heat a darning needle in the flame of a candle. Wipe off the soot and pierce two holes through the main square of each bead just below the triangular points at one end. (For additional help with this project refer to Layering, *pages 88–89*.)

## materials

rainbow, purple, pink, and turquoise
  Friendly Plastic strips

## tools

scissors
nonstick baking parchment and
  baking sheet
tweezers
candle
darning needle

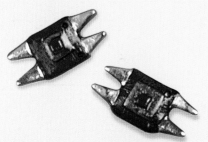

**Opposite:** *These Inca beads may take their inspiration from an ancient culture, but they are transformed here into a contemporary creation. Leather or suede would be an appropriate cord for a necklace or bracelet. (See left for actual bead size.)*

using
**embroidery**

# embroidery techniques

Combine sumptuous fabrics and threads with machine embroidery stitching to create beautiful and unique pieces of jewelry.

### LAYERING

**1 First layer** Strengthen fabric (here red velvet) with fusible webbing and cut out bead shapes. Iron shapes onto a contrasting fabric (here organza) and cut out, leaving a narrow border.

**2 Second layer** When bonding fabrics, iron a piece of fusible webbing onto the first fabric. Remove the backing paper from the webbing, place the second fabric on top and iron to bond.

**3 Stitching** Place the second layer (made in step 2) into an embroidery hoop. Add the first layer on top and embroider around them with straight stitch.

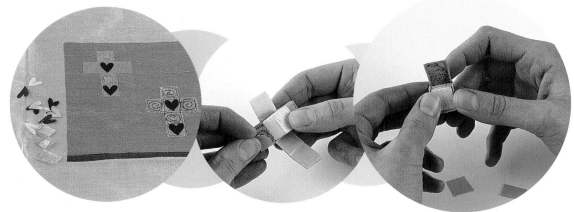

### MAKING SHAPES

**1 Stitching** Attach your bead design to the second layer fabric using the layering method shown above. To fix in place, zigzag stitch around each square.

**2 Balsa base shape** Cut the basic shape of your bead from balsa wood. Pierce a hole through it with an awl. Use double-sided tape to stick the fabric cross to the base shape.

**3 Wrapping the fabric** Carefully wrap the fabric around the wood, pressing firmly and making sure all the edges meet neatly and are securely stuck.

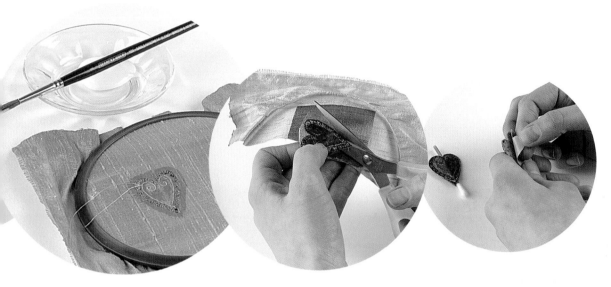

**4 Reinforcing** Turn the hoop over and paint a thin layer of waterproof craft glue over the back of the embroidered shapes, making sure that all the edges are covered, and allow to dry.

**5 Taping** Stick double-sided carpet tape to the backs of the shapes. Cut out the shapes, avoiding the embroidered edging. Peel off the backing paper from the tape.

**6 Joining** Stick your bead shapes together in pairs around a hollow plastic tube (a cotton swab is ideal). Trim the tube to size with a craft knife so that it is concealed within the bead. Decorate edges with seed beads.

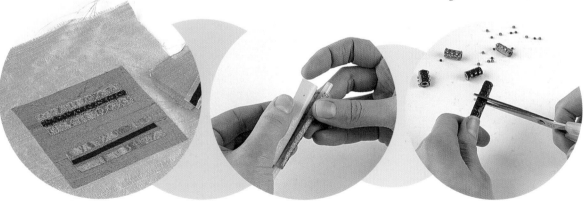

## MAKING TUBULAR BEADS
**1 Stitching** Embroider strips of fabric using the layering method shown above. Here we've used straight stitch to embroider scrolls over the design.

**2 Taping** Apply double-sided tape to the back of the fabric strips. Remove the backing paper from the tape and wrap each strip lengthwise around a drinking straw.

**3 Cutting** Cut each tubular strip into beads of equal length. Embellish the tubes with seed beads, hand stitching them through the surface of the fabric.

# velvet hearts

These sensuous velvet hearts make opulent jewelry. Wear a single heart suspended as a pendant, or a group of them threaded with glass beads to make a languid necklace for a romantic evening.

## materials

fusible webbing
20" x 8" (50cm x 20cm) piece of
  organza
24" (60cm) square of silkscraps
  of red velvet
suitable backing fabric
metallic thread
waterproof craft glue and double-sided
  carpet tape
cotton swabs
seed beads

## tools

scissors and iron
embroidery hoop
sewing machine and sewing needle

Cut a piece of fusible webbing to the same size as the piece of organza. Place the fusible webbing between the organza and the square of silk, and iron to bond. Stretch this fabric into an embroidery hoop, organza face up.

Back the red velvet with fusible webbing, then cut out heart shapes and bond the hearts to the backing fabric. Position the hearts centrally on the organza in the embroidery hoop. Using metallic thread and a sewing machine, embroider a decorative edging around the hearts. Coat the back of the hearts with waterproof craft glue and allow to dry.

Stick double-sided carpet tape to the back of each heart, then cut out the heart shapes. Remove the backing paper from the tape and put pairs of hearts together, sandwiching a hollow plastic tube such as a cotton swab between them. Trim the tube to size. Embellish the beads by hand stitching seed beads around the outside edges. (For additional help with this project refer to Layering, *pages 98–99.*)

**Opposite:** *Tactile and delicate fabrics such as silk, velvet and organza, combined with decorative edging, transform these delicate hearts into romantic Pre-Raphaelite pendants. Try threading one onto a metal choker.*

# bracelet tubes

Fine filigree embroidery and dainty seed beads give these tubular beads their fabulous texture. String them together with glass beads and sequins for an interesting mix of materials.

## materials

fusible webbing
12″ (30cm) square of organza
24″ (60cm) square of silk
four ⅝″ x 9″ (1.5cm x 23cm) strips
  of gold fabric
two ⅜″ x 9″ (1cm x 23cm) strips
  of red fabric
suitable backing fabric
metallic thread
waterproof craft glue
double-sided carpet tape
drinking straws
blue seed beads

## tools

scissors and iron
embroidery hoop, sewing machine,
  and sewing needle

Cut a piece of fusible webbing the same size as the square of organza. Iron the webbing onto the organza, then remove the backing paper and iron the organza onto the square of silk. Stretch the fused fabric into an embroidery hoop, organza face up.

Iron strips of fusible webbing to the back of the gold and red strips, then bond the strips to the backing fabric. Position the strips onto the organza in the embroidery hoop, sandwiching a red strip between pairs of gold. Using metallic thread and a sewing machine, embroider rows of wave-like scrolls along each strip. Coat the back of the strips with waterproof craft glue and allow to dry.

Stick double-sided carpet tape to the back of both wide strips, then cut them out. Remove the backing paper from the tape and wrap the strips lengthwise around drinking straws. Cut them into ¾″ (2cm) lengths and hand stitch seed beads around the tubes in a pleasing arrangement. (For additional help with this project refer to Making tubular beads, *page 99*.)

**Opposite:** *These embroidered tubes, wrapped around sections of drinking straws, sit well against the skin as a bracelet, and with their unusual shape and texture, can form part of a striking design. (See left for actual bead size.)*

# clever cubes

These unique and cleverly designed beads are extremely stylish.
Inside each embroidered case is a cube of balsa wood that holds
the beads firm while being extremely light and easy to work with.

Bond the silk and organza fabrics together with fusible webbing. Using a pencil and ruler, mark out as many identical crosses as you can fit on the organza. The crosses should be 2" (6cm) long, 1½" (3cm) across, and ½" (1.5cm) thick along both arms. Divide each cross into ½" (1.5cm) squares.

Back the red and gold fabric scraps with fusible webbing and cut out small heart shapes. Bond the hearts to the crosses with an iron. Stretch the square of fabric into an embroidery hoop and machine embroider all around the edges and within the vacant squares using metallic thread. Coat the back of the embroidered crosses with waterproof craft glue and allow to dry.

Stick double-sided carpet tape to the back of each cross, then cut them out. Cut ½" (1.5cm) cubes from a rod of balsa wood with a sharp craft knife. Pierce a diagonal hole through each cube using an awl. Remove the backing paper from the tape and place a balsa cube in the center of each cross. Wrap the fabric around the cubes, checking that all the edges are secure. (For additional help with this project refer to Making shapes, *page 98*.)

## materials

12" (30cm) square each of organza
  and silk
fusible webbing
scraps of red velvet and gold fabric
metallic thread
waterproof craft glue and double-sided
  carpet tape
½" (1.5cm) square rod of balsa wood

## tools

scissors and iron
pencil and ruler
embroidery hoop and sewing
  machine
craft knife and awl

**Opposite:** *These exquisite beads have a variety of uses.*
*The contemporary geometric shape of the cube contrasts*
*pleasingly with its cover of silken, embellished fabric.*
*(See left for actual bead size.)*

# using
## your beads

# from beads to jewelry

Try new threads like colored stretch thread or plastic-coated tiger tail, as well as using traditional silk, and waxed threads

The components you will need to transform your handmade beads into pieces of jewelry are known as "findings." These are widely available from bead stores and jewelry suppliers.

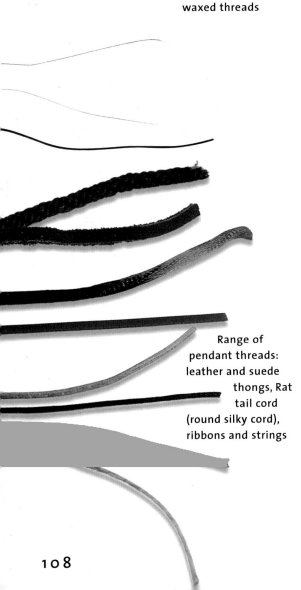

Range of pendant threads: leather and suede thongs, Rat tail cord (round silky cord), ribbons and strings

## threads

If you intend to make a necklace or bracelet, you will need to string your beads together on a length of thread. Threads are available in a variety of materials, including nylon, silk, and wire. The type of thread you use will depend on the weight of the beads, the size of the holes, and whether you want the thread to be visible or not. You also need to decide whether you want to use a clasp to join the ends of the necklace or bracelet together (*see page 109*). If you do not, you must make it long enough to fit over the head or hand, or use elastic thread.

Tiger tail wire is popular for stringing necklaces. Made of twisted fine wires encased in nylon, it is strong and can be used without a needle. However, it is difficult to make a knot in tiger tail wire, so use crimps to secure the ends of the wire instead (*see page 110*). If you are working with fine threads and small beads, you will need to use a beading needle to insert the thread through the holes. Alternately, give the thread a sharp end by dipping it in some glue, wiping off the excess, and then cutting the end

at an angle. If you are making a necklace or bracelet from Friendly Plastic, suitable chains can be bought whole or by length from jewelry suppliers.

Choose a decorative thread for pendant necklaces. Ribbon and cotton cord are good choices because they are inexpensive and washable. Rat tail cord is a round polyester cord with a lovely, silky feel. For a more earthy look, use string, leather, or suede.

## clasps

The clasp is what joins the two halves of the necklace or bracelet securely. There are many different types of clasp available, from those that are plain and functional to fine filigree and ornate diamanté ones. There are also many magnetic clasps available that are much easier to use than traditional ones.

The clasp you choose will depend to a large extent on personal taste, both in terms of the clasp's appearance and how it functions. Other

factors to consider are whether you want the clasp to be seen when the item is worn and also the character of the piece of jewelry to which the clasp will be attached. Once you have strung your bracelet or necklace, look at the finished result carefully and make your choice accordingly—a neat, serious bracelet should not have a fussy fastening, for example; on the other hand, a sparkling, decorative necklace would be spoiled by a dull clasp.

THE FINISHING TOUCH
*Sometimes a necklace calls for a special clasp. This one was chosen because it is reminiscent of underwater treasure troves. The beads were perfect because they looked like bubbles coming out of the fish's mouth.*

## ATTACHING CLASPS

**Threading on the crimp**
If using tiger tail wire, slide the crimp onto the wire and then slide on the catch element of the clasp (a bolt ring is used here). Loop the wire back through the crimp.

**Securing the crimp**
Pull the crimp tight up to the catch without restricting the catch's movement. Use pliers to squeeze the crimp around the thread. If you have special crimping pliers, use the second groove to fold the crimp in half and make a neater finish.

**Finishing off**
Thread a crimp onto the other end of the wire, followed by the clasp. Pull the slack thread in the necklace or bracelet tight so there is no gap, then slide the end of the wire back through the crimp and through the adjacent beads. Squeeze the crimp around the wire as before.

## crimps and bead tips

Crimps are little, round, metal beads that are used to finish the ends of necklaces and bracelets that are strung on tiger tail wire. They are squeezed into the wire to hold the beads and clasp in place because it is difficult to make a secure knot in this type of wire.

Bead tips are available in different sizes and shapes and are used to finish off the ends of necklaces strung on cotton thread. They hide the knots at the ends of the thread to provide a neater, more professional finish. To attach a calotte, simply thread the end of the necklace through the hole in the calotte and tie a knot

as close as you can to the base. Put a little glue onto the knot to make it more secure. Cut away the excess thread and gently squeeze the two halves of the calotte together over the

**Selection of crimps and bead tips**

Selection of head pins and eye pins

knot. The small metal hook or loop on the calotte is for attaching the clasp. Use small clamshell bead tips for fine threads and larger bead tips for thicker threads such as leather, suede, and cotton cord.

## head pins and eye pins

Head pins have a flat "head" at one end and are generally used to make dangle earrings. Beads are threaded onto the pin—the head stops them from sliding off—and then the pin is attached to a hook or other type of earring finding. If the holes in the beads are larger than the head of the pin, thread on a small bead first to stop the rest of the beads from falling off. Eye pins are used in the same way as head pins but they have a loop at one end from which you can hang a drop bead; this will then swing independently from the rest of the earring. Head pins and eye pins are usually available in three lengths.

## earring findings

Findings for pierced ears are either studs or hooks. Studs are small two-part findings consisting of a straight rod of metal that goes through the ear and either a butterfly or bullet

clutch at the back to secure the rod in place. The rod may have a flat front onto which a bead can be stuck or a loop from which to hang a head or eye pin. Hooks all have loops at the front that hang below the earlobe and onto which a head or eye pin can be attached. Some have a small loop at the back to prevent the hooks from falling out of the ear.

The options for unpierced ears are clip-ons and screw-backs. These are more comfortable than they used to be, with rubber and plastic backing cushions. They have a little loop at the front and sometimes a cabochon mount.

Earring findings are available in many different metals, including gold, silver, and copper. Hypoallergenic niobium and titanium findings are also available and come in green, turquoise, blue, and purple colors.

Findings for pierced ears

Findings for unpierced ears

## MAKING DANGLE EARRINGS

### Threading the beads

Choose a bead that is not too large or heavy and thread it onto a head pin. If the hole in the bead is larger than the head of the pin, thread on a small bead first. Thread more small beads onto the head pin, but make sure that you leave the end of the pin unbeaded.

### Forming a loop

Use needle-nose pliers to bend back the wire at the end of the head pin to form a loop as close to the beads as possible. Cut off any wire in excess of ½" (1cm), then close the loop using the tips of pliers. Trim off more wire if necessary.

### Attaching the finding

Hook the beaded head pin onto the loop of the earring finding. Close the loop securely using pliers, but take care not to do it too tightly—the head pin should be able to move freely.

Although the basic types of earring findings are easy to categorize, the range of different styles available is enormous. Try not to get too bogged down with decision-making. The finding itself needs to be unobtrusive. Choose a color—gold, silver, black, or titanium—that works well with the color of the beads you are using. Whether you choose real gold or silver depends on how much money you want to spend. All types of metal work equally well, although it is important to know whether you are allergic to any metals, in which case you should always use hypoallergenic findings made from niobium or titanium.

There are a number of things to consider when making beads for earrings. Comfort is most important, so always choose beads that are not too heavy. The length and shape of the beads will depend on the shape of your face and your hairstyle. Hold the beads up to a mirror to find what suits you best. If you choose to make dangle earrings, remember that they need to swing freely, so take care not to make the connecting loop too tight (see above).

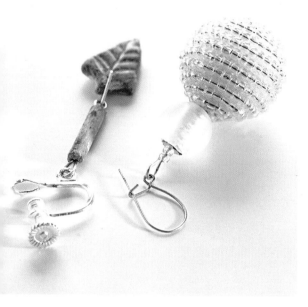

## HOOK FINDINGS

The beads shown here were used because they are lightweight yet durable. The screw-back finding on the left is for unpierced ears and may be a bit more secure than the clip-on findings often used for unpierced ears. Some earring findings, such as the hooks for pierced ears on the right, clip into a loop behind the ear in order to stop them from falling off easily.

## STUD FINDINGS

Stud findings are suitable for pierced ears. They consist of male and female components. The rod or post (male) fits through the ear and is held in place by a butterfly or bullet clutch (female) at the back of the ear. Once again, lightweight, durable beads are best, both in terms of comfort when wearing them and being less liable to fall out.

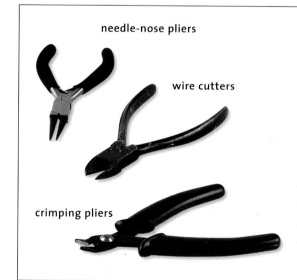

needle-nose pliers

wire cutters

crimping pliers

## PLIERS

Needle-nose pliers are essential for making earrings. They have tapered points that enable different sizes of loop to be formed. Wire cutters are also very useful because they allow you to get close in to where you want to cut. If you do not have wire cutters, use the cutting edges of a pair of pliers. Crimping pliers are worth investing in if you are going to make lots of necklaces. They have two grooves: the first for squeezing the crimp and the second for folding it neatly. Otherwise, use ordinary pliers.

# bracelets

Bracelets are a fun way to use your beads, especially if you have only made a few. String them onto elastic cord to make them easy to wear, and create matching rings, necklaces, and earrings.

EMBROIDERED TUBE BRACELETS

*These slender tubes are perfect for a bracelet. Opulent yet lightweight, they lie comfortably against the skin and you can wear several in contrasting colors.*

With the advent of elastic cords, bracelet-making has become simpler than ever. The cord is available many different colors and several thicknesses. When tying the elastic, make sure it is secure or you will risk losing your beads. Tie the first knot very tight, then tie a second knot. Put a little glue onto the knot to make it really secure.

When making bracelets, remember that the beads lie next to the skin, so they need to be comfortable and not get in the way of your hands. In the examples pictured here, the embroidered tube bracelets have been interspersed with sequins and small beads, making a lightweight bracelet full of vibrancy and interesting textures. The ladybug and spider beads are disk-shaped so that they lie flat and comfortably against the wrist. There are two parallel holes through each bead to prevent them from swiveling around and facing the wrong way.

In the duck bracelet, a single cane bead featuring a swimming duck has been used as a centerpiece and teamed with smaller wooden beads. Cane beads can look too bulky and feel uncomfortable against the wrist if strung all together, so it is better to use them as a feature—the matching ring helps to highlight the eye-catching birds.

DUCK BEADS (RIGHT)

*Make a matching set of jewelry using cane beads featuring a duck or other design of your choice. A necklace could easily be made to go with this bracelet and ring, and smaller duck beads could be glued onto earring findings.*

BUG BEADS (BELOW)

*Whether you choose to make colorful ladybug beads or friendly spiders, they can both be strung onto elastic cord to make charming, easy-to-wear bracelets.*

# necklaces

When using your beads to make necklaces, play around with different combinations and try mixing them with plain store-bought beads to highlight the individuality of your own creations.

When making a necklace, always have a mirror at hand so that you can look at different combinations against your skin. Some beads only look good on short necklaces; others need space to move about. Take into account the garments you want to wear with the necklace and the occasions you will wear it. These considerations will all help determine your design, and trial and error is the best way to achieve success.

HEART PENDANT (*ABOVE*)
*Use wire or a metal choker to suspend a single embroidered heart bead. Here, the heart has been attached to the wire using beaded thread, which forms an attractive loop around the wire, and a tassel at the base of the heart. The contrast between the sleek wire and the sumptuous velvet is stunning.*

FISH NECKLACE (*LEFT*)
*For this necklace to hang well the fish beads required large spaces between them. The tiny glass beads compliment the fish and give a lighter, modern appearance to the necklace.*

# pendants

To make a pendant necklace, you need a way of suspending the bead from the cord or ribbon. Do this by threading the bead onto a head pin in the same way as Making dangle earrings (*see pages 112–113*). You may need to thread a smaller base bead below the main bead and some above it if the main bead's hole is large. Use needle-nose pliers to form a loop at the end of the head pin large enough to accommodate the cord. The simplest way to fasten a pendant necklace is to tie the two ends of the cord together in a reef knot. If you would prefer a neater finish, use a box calotte and a suitable clasp (*see pages 109–110.*)

SELECTION OF PENDANTS

*Any large bead can be used on its own to make a pendant if you choose a suitable thread or cord from which to hang it. From left to right: rat tail cord, suede thong, leather thong, string of imitation ivory beads, twisted strings of seed beads, and suede again.*

# color, shape, and scale

The range of colors and shapes available to the bead maker is huge. You can also combine different sizes of beads with dramatic effects. Here are some combinations to inspire your creativity.

## jeweled tassel

The soft, flowing abundance of this silky tassel combined with the bejeweled and encrusted bead makes a stunning statement. Use it in a bathroom as a light pull cord or tieback, or to complement a sumptuous bathrobe. The cool silver beads hide the wire fixture at the top of the tassel when it is hanging.

## to make the tassel

Use a store-bought silk tassel (you may need to remove some of the head detail, but make sure that the strands are still securely attached). Bind strong thread tightly through the middle of the tassel and fasten it securely to an eye pin (*see page 111.*) Thread the pin through the main bead and through the loop in the cord from

which you will hang the tassel. Use needle-nose
pliers to bend the wire back and into the bead.
Buy or make beads with a wide aperture and
thread them over the cord to hide the loop of
the eye pin at the top of the main bead of the
tassel. Alternately, wrap stranded floss
(embroidery thread) around the end of the
cord to hide the wire loop.

### CUBE BRACELET

*This clever and unconventional bracelet uses square
beads strung diagonally on elastic cord. The hot red
and rich metallic embroidery of the cubes contrasts
well with the cool turquoise and bronze beads between
them. The difference in size between the main beads
and those interspersing them gives this dramatic
bracelet even more impact.*

## heart necklace

The contrast between the hard red glass beads and the soft velvet of the hearts is extremely effective in this lovely, languid, and romantic necklace.

## to make the necklace

Suspend a single heart to hang as a pendant to mid-chest length (*see page 117*), then attach the pendant to some wire, thread, or cord. Thread a mixture of beads onto the wire on each side of the central heart for approximately 2″ (5cm), then add a pair of hearts. Repeat until you have seven hearts, making sure you create a symmetrical arrangement. This section of the necklace will be positioned at your collar bone. Finish the necklace with glass beads and choose a suitable sophisticated clasp to complete the design (*see pages 109–110.*)

## sun-bleached tassel

The simple plain cotton tassel and the chunky terra-cotta beads make a very natural combination. The distressed paintwork on the beads teamed with the natural rope gives the tassel a seaside feel that is suitable for use in a bathroom as a light pull cord or tieback.

## to make the tassel

Cut a 10″ (25cm) length of thick cotton rope and bind it tightly around the middle with strong thread. Pass the thread through a large, chunky bead and bind it tightly to a double length of ¼″ (5mm) thick cotton cord. Unweave the strands of the rope to form a tassel.

DELICATE CHAIN (*RIGHT*)
*Lengths of chain can be bought from jewelry supply stores, or you could use a chain you already have. Use jump rings to suspend pretty Friendly Plastic heart beads to make a light and cheerful necklace. Make matching earrings by sticking hearts onto stud findings or hanging them from hooks. The contrasting silver, gold, pink, and red colors work well together because they share a metallic gleam.*

# mixing materials

Materials often look best when combined with contrasting ones—soft against hard, light against heavy, rough against smooth. This helps to highlight the beads and create sensuous jewelry.

Once you have made your beads, the best way to decide which materials to combine them with is simply to look around you for inspiration. Look at the other objects you have in your home, in your workplace, and in your local area. Another good idea is to take your homemade beads to your nearest bead supplier and hold them up next to some of the beads in the store (make sure the store owner is aware of what you are doing). Different combinations will reveal different qualities in the materials. If you do not have a bead supplier near you, look for one in your local telephone directory or refer to the list of resources (*see page 124*). Ask the companies to send you a catalog—it's the next best thing to visiting a bead store.

Remember that the object of the exercise is to complement your homemade beads, not to

overwhelm them. Always try to avoid beads that will dwarf your own, and choose colors that are sympathetic. Consider also where the materials originally came from. For instance, when making a necklace of slate beads, white wire is a good choice because it mimics the natural strata lines found in the stone. The slate can be teamed with frosted glass beads to echo its seaworn feel.

The most important thing to remember is that there are no hard-and-fast rules—if you like it, use it.

### BEADED BAUBLES (LEFT)

*The granular texture of the main baubles of this necklace contrasts beautifully with the ultra-glossy beads that divide them. The small beads allow space between the large baubles but do not compete with them. The intense colors of the small beads add a tanginess to the subtle sherbet colors of the baubles.*

### CLAY AND GLASS STRINGS (RIGHT)

*The light airiness of the subtly colored glass beads contrasts well with the heavy bulkiness of the clay hearts and birds. A glass disk at the top of the string of bird beads gives emphasis, like a capital letter at the beginning of a sentence—all you have to do is search for something similar for the other end to add a full point.*

# resources

## US

You can find herbs and essential oils at your local food health store. See general craft stores for polymer clays and Friendly Plastic.

## GENERAL CRAFT

General Craft
Hobby Lobby
7707 SW 44th Street
Oklahoma City, OK 73179
Tel: (405) 745 1100
www.hobbylobby.com

Michaels Arts and Crafts
8000 Bent Branch Road
Irving, TX 75063
Tel: (214) 409 1300
www.michaels.com

## BEADS, FINDINGS, THREADS, WIRES, FABRIC, EMBELLISHMENTS

Beadworks® Group
North American General Offices:
Westcroft Beadworks, Inc. and Beadworks
International, Inc.
149 Water Street
Norwalk, CT 06854
Tel: (203) 852 9108
Fax: (203) 855 8015
www.beadworks.com
*Beads from around the world, including glass beads, African beads, findings, sterling findings, and charms.*

Beadworks® (individual store)
290 Thayer Store
Providence, RI 02906
Tel: (401) 861 4540

Jo-Ann Fabrics
Customer Care
841 Apollo Street
Suite 350
El Segundo, CA 90245
www.joann.com
Toll free: 1 888 739 4120

Hancock Fabrics
2711 El Camino
Sacramento, CA 95821
Tel: (916) 484 7751
www.hancockfabrics.com

*See your local fabric store to find unspun yarn.*

## METALS

Metalliferous
34 West 46th Street
New York, NY 10036
Tel: (212) 944 0909
Toll-free: 1 888 944 0909
Fax: (212) 944 0644
www.metalliferous.com
Email: metals@metalliferous.com
*A full service, fully-stocked supplier of metal, tools, and supplies to jewelers, crafters, hobbyists, metalworkers, sculptors.*

Swest Inc.
11090 N. Stemmons Freeway
P.O. Box 59389
Dallas, TX 75229-1389
Tel: (214) 247 7744
Toll-free order: 1 800 527 5057
Fax: 1 800 441 5162
Email: email@swestinc.com
*Czech glass beads, stone beads, metal beads, base metal,*
*beading supplies, tools, findings, precious metals and wire.*

## UK

### BEADS AND JEWELRY FINDINGS

Bead Exclusive
4 Samara Park
Cavalier Road
Heathfield
Newton Abbot
Devon TQ12 6TR
Tel: (01626) 834 934
Fax: (01626) 834 787

The Bead Shop
21 Tower Street
London WC2H 9NF
Tel: (020) 7240 0931
www.beadworks.co.uk

Ells and Farrier
20 Beak Street
London W1R 3HA
Tel: (020) 7629 9964

### FLEECE

The Handweavers Studio and Gallery Ltd
29 Haroldstone Road
London E17 7AN
Tel: (020) 8521 2281

### FIMO AND FRIENDLY PLASTIC

Fred Aldons
P.O. Box 135
37 Lever Street
Manchester M1 1LW
Tel: (0161) 236 2477

### HERBS, SPICES, AND AROMATIC OILS

G. Baldwin & Co.
171–173 Walworth Road
London SE17 1RW
Tel: (020) 7703 5550

Neal's Yard Remedies
15 Neal's Yard
London WC2 9DP
Tel: (020) 7379 7222
Fax: (020) 7379 0705
www.nealsyardremedies.co.uk

# index

# credits

Thanks to Siân Irvine for her stylish
photography and to Emma Baxter, the editor;
to Jo Collon for the Friendly Plastic projects
(*pages 86–95*); to Vicki King for the embroidery
projects (*pages 96–105*); to Victoria Brown for the
spotted, striped, and Disco Diva beads and
to Dawn Simmons for the Psychedelic beads
in the felt chapter (*pages 46–55*).